RUBÁIYÁT OF DOC SIFERS
BY JAMES WHITCOMB RILEY

Other Books by
James Whitcomb Riley

POEMS HERE AT HOME.
NEGHBORLY POEMS.
SKETCHES IN PROSE AND OCCASIONAL VERSES.
AFTERWHILES.
PIPES O' PAN (Prose and Verse).
RHYMES OF CHILDHOOD.
FLYING ISLANDS OF THE NIGHT.
OLD-FASHIONED ROSES (English Edition).
GREEN FIELDS AND RUNNING BROOKS.
ARMAZINDY.
A CHILD-WORLD.
AN OLD SWEETHEART OF MINE.

RUBÁIYÁT OF DOC SIFERS

BY JAMES WHITCOMB RILEY

ILLUSTRATED
BY
C. M. RELYEA

PUBLISHED BY THE CENTURY CO.
NEW YORK MDCCCXCVII

THE DE VINNE PRESS.

TO

DR. FRANKLIN W. HAYS

THE LOYAL CHUM OF MY LATEST YOUTH
AND LIKE FRIEND AND COMRADE STILL
WITH ALL GRATEFUL AFFECTION OF

THE AUTHOR.

RUBÁIYÁT OF DOC SIFERS
BY JAMES WHITCOMB RILEY

WE FOUND him in that Far-away that yet to us seems near—
We vagrants of but yesterday when idlest youth was here,—
When lightest song and laziest mirth possessed us through and through,
And all the dreamy summer-earth seemed drugged with morning dew:

When our ambition scarce had shot a stalk or blade indeed:
Yours,—choked as in the garden-spot you still deferred to "weed":
Mine,—but a pipe half-cleared of pith—as now it flats and whines
In sympathetic cadence with a hiccough in the lines.

Aye, even then—O timely hour!—the High Gods did confer
In our behalf:—And, clothed in power, lo, came their Courier—
Not winged with flame nor shod with wind,—but ambling down the pike,
Horseback, with saddlebags behind, and guise all human-like.

X

And it was given us to see, beneath his rustic rind,
A native force and mastery of such inspiring kind,
That half unconsciously we made obeisance.—Smiling, thus
His soul shone from his eyes and laid its glory over us.

. . . . . .

Though, faring still that Far-away that yet to us seems near,
His form, through mists of yesterday, fades from the vision here,
Forever as he rides, it is in retinue divine,—
The hearts of all his time are his, with your hale heart and mine.

RUBÁIYÁT OF DOC SIFERS

BY JAMES WHITCOMB RILEY

I

RUBÁIYÁT OF DOC SIFERS

I

EF you don't know DOC SIFERS I 'll jes argy, here and now,
You 've bin a mighty little while about here, anyhow!
'Cause Doc he 's rid these roads and woods -- er *swum* 'em, now and then —
And practised in this neighberhood sence hain't no tellin' when!

II

In radius o' fifteen mile'd, all p'ints o' compass round,
No man er woman, chick er child, er team, on top o' ground,
But knows *him* — yes, and got respects and likin' fer him, too,
Fer all his so-to-speak dee-fects o' genius showin' through!

III

Some claims he 's absent-minded; some has said they wuz afeard
To take his powders when he come and dosed 'em out, and 'peared
To have his mind on somepin' else — like County Ditch, er some
New way o' tannin' mussrat-pelts, er makin' butter come.

IV

He 's cur'ous — they hain't no mistake about
it! — but he 's got
Enough o' extry brains to make a *jury* — like
as not.
They 's no *describin'* Sifers,— fer, when all is
said and done,
He 's jes *hisse'f Doc Sifers* — ner they hain't
no other one!

V

Doc 's allus sociable, polite, and 'greeable, you-
'll find —
Pervidin' ef you strike him right and nothin'
on his mind,—
Like in some *hurry*, when they 've sent fer
Sifers *quick*, you see,
To 'tend some sawmill-accident, er picnic jam-
boree;

VI

Er when the lightnin' 's struck some hare-
    brained harvest-hand; er in
Some 'tempt o' suicidin' — where they 'd ort
    to try ag'in!
I 've *knowed* Doc haul up from a trot and
    talk a' hour er two
When railly he 'd a-ort o' not a-stopped fer
    "*Howdy-do!*"

VII

And then, I 've met him 'long the road, *a-*
lopin',— starin' straight
Ahead,— and yit he never knowed me when
I hollered "*Yatc,*
Old Saddlebags!" all hearty-like, er "*Who*
you goin' to kill?"
And he 'd say nothin'— only hike on faster,
starin' still!

VIII

I 'd bin insulted, many a time, ef I jes wuz n't
shore
Doc did n't mean a thing. And I 'm not
tetchy any more
Sence that-air day, ef he 'd a-jes a-stopped to
jaw with *me*,
They 'd bin a little dorter less in my own
fambily!

IX

Times *now,* at home, when Sifers' name comes up, I jes *let on,*
You know, 'at *I* think Doc 's to *blame,* the way he 's bin and gone
And disapp'inted folks—'Ll-*jee*-mun-*nee!* you 'd ort to then
Jes hear my wife light into me—"*ongrateful-est o' men!*"

X

'Mongst *all* the women—mild er rough, splendifferous er plain,
Er them *with* sense, er not enough to come in out the rain,—
Jes ever' shape and build and style o' women, fat er slim—
They all like Doc, and got a smile and pleasant word fer *him!*

XI

Ner hain't no horse I 've ever saw but what 'll neigh and try
To sidle up to him, and paw, and sense him, ear-and-eye:
Then jes a tetch o' Doc's old pa'm, to pat 'em, er to shove
Along their nose—and they 're as ca'm as any cooin' dove!

XII

And same with *dogs*,—take any breed, er strain, er pedigree,
Er racial caste 'at can't concede no use fer you er me,—
They 'll putt all predju-dice aside in *Doc's* case and go in
Kahoots with him, as satisfied as he wuz kith-and-kin!

XIII

And Doc 's a wonder, trainin' pets!—He 's got a chicken-hawk,
In kind o' half-cage, where he sets out in the gyarden-walk,
And got that wild bird trained so tame, he 'll loose him, and he 'll fly
Clean to the woods!—Doc calls his name—and he 'll come, by-and-by!

XIV

Some says no money down ud buy that bird
o' Doc.—Ner no
Inducement to the *bird*, says I, 'at *he 'd* let
Sifers go!
And Doc *he* say 'at *he 's* content—long as
a bird o' prey
Kin 'bide *him*, it 's a *compliment*, and takes
it thataway.

XV

But, gittin' back to *docterin'*—all the sick and
in distress,
And old and pore, and weak and small, and
lone and motherless,—
I jes tell *you* I 'preciate the man 'at 's got
the love
To "go ye forth and ministrate!" as Scriptur'
tells us of.

XVI

Dull times, Doc jes *mi*anders round, in that old
rig o' his:
And hain't no tellin' where he 's bound ner
guessin' where he is;
He 'll drive, they tell, jes thataway fer maybe
six er eight
Days at a stretch; and neighbers say he 's
bin clean round the State.

XVII

He picked a' old tramp up, one trip, 'bout
eighty mile'd from here,
And fetched him home and k-yored his hip,
and kep' him 'bout a year;
And feller said—in all *his* ja'nts round this
terreschul ball
'At no man wuz a *circumstance* to *Doc!*—he
topped 'em all!—

XVIII

Said, bark o' trees 's a' open book to Doc, and
vines and moss
He read like writin'—with a look knowed ever'
dot and cross:
Said, stars at night wuz jes as good 's a com-
pass: said, he s'pose
You could n't lose Doc in the woods the
darkest night that blows!

XIX

Said, Doc 'll tell you, purty clos't, by under-
bresh and plants,
How fur off *warter* is,—and 'most perdict the
sort o' chance
You 'll have o' findin' *fish;* and how they 're
liable to *bite,*
And whether they 're a-bitin' now, er only
after night.

XX

And, whilse we 're talkin' *fish*,—I mind they
formed a fishin'-crowd
(When folks *could* fish 'thout gittin' *fined*, and
seinin' wuz allowed!)
O' leadin' citizens, you know, to go and seine
"Old Blue"—
But had n't no big seine, and so—w'y, what
wuz they to do? . . .

XXI

And Doc he say he thought 'at *he* could *knit*
a stitch er two—
"Bring the *materials* to me—'at 's all I 'm
astin' you!"
And down he sets—six weeks, i jing! and
knits that seine plum done—
Made corks too, brails and ever'thing—good
as a boughten one!

XXII

Doc 's *public* sperit — when the sick 's not takin' *all* his time
And he 's got *some* fer politics — is simple yit sublime :—
He 'll *talk* his *principles* — and they air *honest ;* — but the sly
Friend strikes him first, election-day, he 'd 'commodate, er die !

XXIII

And yit, though Doc, as all men knows, is square straight up and down,
That vote o' his is — well, I s'pose — the cheapest one in town ; —
A fact 'at 's sad to verify, as could be done on oath —
I 've voted Doc myse'f — *And I was criminal fer both !*

XXIV

You kin corrupt the *ballot-box*—corrupt *your-se'f*, as well—
Corrupt *some* neighbers,—but old Doc 's as oncorruptible
As Holy Writ. So putt a pin right there!—Let *Sifers* be,
I jucks! he would n't vote agin his own worst inimy!

XXV

When Cynthy Eubanks laid so low with fever, and Doc Glenn
Told Euby Cynth 'ud haf to go—they sends fer *Sifers* then! . . .
Doc sized the case: "She 's starved," says he, "fer *warter*—yes, and *meat!*
The treatment 'at she 'll git from *me* 's all she kin drink and eat!"

XXVI

He orders Euby then to split some wood, and take and build
A fire in kitchen-stove, and git a young spring-chicken killed;
And jes whirled in and th'owed his hat and coat there on the bed,
And warshed his hands and sailed in that-air kitchen, Euby said,

XXVII

And biled that chicken-broth, and got that dinner — all complete
And clean and crisp and good and hot as mortal ever eat!
And Cynth and Euby both 'll say 'at Doc 'll git as good
Meals-vittles up, jes any day, as any *woman* could!

XXVIII

Time Sister Abbick tuk so bad with striffen
o' the lung,
P'tracted Meetin', where she had jes shouted,
prayed and sung
All winter long, through snow and thaw,—
when Sifers come, says he:
"No, M'lissy; don't poke out your raw and
cloven tongue at me!—

XXIX

"I know, without no symptoms but them
injarubber-shoes
You promised me to never putt a fool-foot in
ner use
At purril o' your life!" he said. "And I
won't save you *now*,
Onless—here on your dyin' bed—you con-
secrate your vow!"

XXX

Without a-claimin' *any creed*, Doc's rail religious views
Nobody knows—ner got no *need* o' knowin' whilse he choose
To be heerd not of man, ner raise no loud, vainglorious prayers
In crowded marts, er public ways, er—i jucks, *any*wheres!—

XXXI

'Less 'n it *is* away deep down in his own heart, at night,
Facin' the storm, when all the town 's a-sleepin' snug and tight —
Him splashin' hence from scenes o' pride and sloth and gilded show,
To some pore sufferer's bedside o' anguish, don't you know!

XXXII

Er maybe dead o' *winter* — makes no odds to *Doc*, — he 's got
To face the weather ef it takes the hide off! 'cause he 'll not
Lie out o' goin' and p'tend he 's sick hisse'f — like *some*
'At I could name 'at folks might send fer and they 'd *never* come!

XXXIII

Like pore Phin Hoover — when he goes to
that last dance o' his!
That Chris'mus when his feet wuz froze — and
Doc saved all they is
Left of 'em — "'Nough," as Phin say now,
"to *track* me by, and be
A adver*tise*ment, anyhow, o' what Doc 's done
fer me! —

XXXIV

"When *he* come — knife-and-saw" — Phin say,
"I knowed, ef I 'd the spunk,
'At Doc 'ud fix me up *some* way, ef nothin'
but my *trunk*
Wuz left, he 'd fasten *casters* in, and have
me, spick-and-span,
A-skootin' round the streets ag'in as spry as
any man!"

XXXV

Doc sees a patient 's *got* to quit—he 'll ease him down serene
As dozin' off to sleep, and yit not dope him with mor-*pheen.*—
He won't tell *what*—jes 'lows 'at he has "airn't the right to sing
'O grave, where is thy victery! O death, where is thy sting!'"

XXXVI

And, mind ye now!—it 's not in scoff and scorn, by long degree,
'At Doc gits things like that-un off: it 's jes his *shority*
And total faith in Life to Come,—w'y, "from that *Land o' Bliss*,"
He says, "we 'll haf to chuckle some, a-lookin' back at this!"

XXXVII

And, still in p'int, I mind, one *night o' 'niti-*
ation at
Some secert lodge, 'at Doc set right down on
'em, square and flat,
When they mixed up some Scriptur' and wuz
funnin'-like — w'y, he
Lit in 'em with a rep'imand 'at ripped 'em,
A to Z!

XXXVIII

And onc't — when gineral loafin'-place wuz
old Shoe-Shop — and all
The gang 'ud git in there and brace their
backs ag'inst the wall
And *settle* questions that had went onsettled
long enough,—
Like "wuz no Heav'n — ner no torment" —
jes talkin' awful rough!

XXXIX

There wuz Sloke Haines and old Ike Knight
and Coonrod Simmes — all three
Ag'inst the Bible and the Light, and scoutin'
Deity.
"*Science*," says Ike, "it *dimonstrates* — it
takes nobody's word —
Scriptur' er not,— it *'vestigates* ef sich things
could occurred!"

XL

Well, Doc he heerd this, — he 'd drapped in
a minute, fer to git
A tore-off heel pegged on agin,— and, as he
stood on it
And stomped and grinned, he says to Ike,
"I s'pose now, purty soon
Some lightnin'-bug, indignant-like, 'll ''vesti-
gate' the moon! . . . .

XLI

"No, Ike," says Doc, "this world hain't saw
no brains like yourn and mine
With sense enough to grasp a law 'at takes a
brain divine.—
I 've bared the thoughts of brains in doubt,
and felt their finest pulse,—
And mortal brains jes won't turn out omni-
potent results!"

XLII

And Doc he 's got respects to spare the *rich*
as well as *pore*—
Says he, "I 'd turn no *millionaire* onsheltered
from my door."—
Says he, "What 's wealth to him in quest o'
honest friends to back
And love him fer *hisse'f?*—not jes because
he 's made his jack!"

XLIII

And childern.— *Childern?* Lawzy-day! Doc
worships 'em!—You call
Round at his house and *ast* 'em!—they 're
a-*swarmin'* there—that 's all!—
They 're in his *Lib*'ry—in best room—in
kitchen—fur and near,—
In office too, and, I p'sume, his operatin'-
cheer!

XLIV

You know they 's men 'at *bees* won't sting?—
They 's plaguey *few*, — but Doc
He 's one o' *them*. — And same, i jing! with
childern; — they jes flock
Round Sifers *natchurl!* — in his lap, and in
his pockets, too,
And in his old fur mitts and cap, and *heart* as
warm and true!

XLV

It 's cur'ous, too, — 'cause Doc hain't got no
childern of his own —
'Ceptin' the ones he 's tuk and brought up,
'at 's bin left alone
And orphans when their father died, er mo-
ther, — and Doc he
Has he'pped their dyin' satisfied. — "The child
shall live with me

XLVI

"And Winniferd, my wife," he 'd say, and stop right there, and cle'r
His th'oat, and go on thinkin' way *some* mother-hearts down here
Can't never feel *their own* babe's face a-pressin' 'em, ner make
Their naked breasts a restin'-place fer any baby's sake.

XLVII

Doc's *Li*b'ry — as he calls it, — well, they 's ha'f-a-dozen she'ves
Jam-full o' books — I could n't tell *how* many — count yourse'ves!
One whole she'f's Works on Medicine! and most the rest 's about
First Settlement, and Indians in here, — 'fore we driv 'em out. —

XLVIII

And Plutarch's Lives — and life also o' Dan'el Boone, and this-
Here Mungo Park, and Adam Poe — jes all the *lives* they is!
And Doc 's got all the *novels* out, — by Scott and Dickison
And Cooper. — And, I make no doubt, he 's read 'em ever' one!

Doc's Lib'ry

XLIX

Onc't, in his office, settin' there, with crowd
o' eight er nine
Old neighbers with the time to spare, and
Doc a-feelin' fine,
A man rid up from Rollins, jes fer Doc to
write him out
Some blame p'scription — done, I guess, in
minute, nigh about.—

L

And *I* says, "Doc, you 'pear so spry, jes
write me that recei't
You have fer bein' *happy* by,—fer that 'u'd
shorely beat
Your *medicine!*" says I.—And quick as *s'cat!*
Doc turned and writ
And handed me: "Go he'p the sick, and putt
your heart in it."

LI

And then, "A-talkin' furder 'bout that line
o' thought," says he,
"Ef we 'll jes do the work cut out and give'
to you and me,
We 'll lack no joy, ner appetite, ner all we 'd
ort to eat,
And sleep like childern ever' night—as puore
and ca'm and sweet."

LII

Doc *has* bin 'cused o' *offishness* and lack o' talkin' free
And extry friendly; but he says, "I 'm *'feard* o' talk," says he,—
"I 've got," he says, "a natchurl turn fer talkin' fit to kill.—
The best and hardest thing to learn is trick o' keepin' still."

LIII

Doc *kin* smoke, and I s'pose he *might* drink licker — jes fer fun.
He says, "*You* smoke, *you* drink all right; but *I* don't — neether one" —
Says, "I *like* whiskey — 'good old rye' — but like it in its place,
Like that-air warter in your eye, er nose there on your face."

LIV

Doc 's bound to have his joke! The day he got that off on me
I jes had sold a load o' hay at "Scofield's Livery,"
And tolled Doc in the shed they kep' the hears't in, where I 'd hid
The stuff 'at got me "out o' step," as Sifers said it did.

LV

Doc hain't, to say, no "*rollin' stone*," and yit he hain't no hand
Fer '*cumulatin'*.—*Home* 's his own, and scrap o' farmin'-land—
Enough to keep him out the way when folks is tuk down sick
The suddentest—'most any day they want him 'special quick.

LVI

And yit Doc loves his practice; ner don't, wilful, want to slight
No call — no matter who — how fur away — er day er night.—
He loves his work — he loves his friends — June, Winter, Fall, and Spring:
His *lovin'* — facts is — never ends; he loves jes *ever*'thing. . . .

LVII

'Cept — *keepin' books.* He never sets down no accounts. — He hates,
The worst of all, collectin' debts — the worst, the more he waits. —
I 've knowed him, when at last he *had* to dun a man, to end
By makin' him a loan — and mad he had n't more to lend.

LVIII

When Pence's Drug Store ust to be in full
blast, they wuz some
Doc's patients got things frekantly there,
charged to him, i gum!—
Doc run a bill there, don't you know, and allus
when he squared,
He never questioned nothin',—so he had his
feelin's spared.

LIX

Now sich as that, I hold and claim, hain't
'*scusable*—it 's not
Perfessional!—It 's jes a shame 'at Doc his-
se'f hain't got
No better *business*-sense! That 's why lots 'd
respect him more,
And not give him the clean go-by fer *other*
doctors. Shore!

PENCES
STORE

LX

This-here Doc *Glenn*, fer instance; er this little jack-leg *Hall;*—
They 're *business*—folks respects 'em fer their *business* more 'n all
They ever knowed, er ever *will*, 'bout *medicine.*—Yit they
Collect their money, k-yore er kill.—They 're *business*, anyway!

LXI

You ast Jake Dunn;—he 's worked it out in *figgers.*—He kin show
Stastistics how Doc 's airnt about *three* fortunes in a row,—
Ever' ten-year' hand-runnin' straight—*three* of 'em—*thirty* year'
'At Jake kin count and 'lucidate o' Sifers' practice here.

LXII

Yit—"Praise the Lord," says Doc, "we 've got our little home!" says he—
"(It 's railly *Winniferd's*, but what she owns, she sheers with me.)
We' got our little gyarden-spot, and peach- and apple-trees,
And stable, too, and chicken-lot, and eighteen hive' o' bees."

LXIII

You call it anything you please, but it 's
witchcraft—the power
'At Sifers has o' handlin' bees!—He 'll watch
'em by the hour—
Mix right amongst 'em, mad and hot and
swarmin'!—yit they won't
Sting *him*, er *want* to—*'pear* to not,—at least
I know they *don't*.

LXIV

With *me* and bees they 's no *p'tense* o' social-
bility—
A dad-burn bee 'u'd climb a fence to git a
whack at *me!*
I s'pose no thing 'at 's *got* a sting is railly
satisfied
It 's *sharp* enough, ontel, i jing! he 's honed
it on my hide!

LXV

And Doc he 's allus had a knack *inventin'*
things.— Dee-vised
A windlass wound its own se'f back as it run
down: and s'prised
Their new hired girl with *clothes-line,* too, and
clothes-pins, all in *one:*
Purt'-nigh all left fer *her* to do wuz git her
primpin' done!

LXVI

And onc't, I mind, in airly Spring, and tappin'
sugar-trees,
Doc made a dad-burn little thing to sharpen
spiles with — these-
Here wood'-spouts 'at the peth 's punched out,
and driv' in where they bore
The auger-holes. He sharpened 'bout *a mil-
lion* spiles er more!

LXVII

And Doc 's the first man ever swung a *bucket*
on a tree
Instid o' *troughs;* and first man brung *grained*
sugar — so 's 'at he
Could use it fer his coffee, and fer cookin',
don't you know.—
Folks come clean up from Pleasantland 'fore
they 'd *believe* it, though!

LXVIII

And all Doc's stable-doors *on*locks and locks
theirse'ves — and gates
The same way; — all rigged up like clocks, with
pulleys, wheels, and weights,—
So, 's Doc says, "drivin' *out*, er *in*, they 'll
open; and they 'll *then*,
All quiet-like, shet up ag'in like little gentle-
men!"

LXIX

And Doc 'ud made a mighty good *detective.*—
Neighbers all
Will testify to *that* — er *could*, ef they wuz
legal call:
His theories on any crime is worth your
listenin' to.—
And he has hit 'em, many a time, 'long 'fore
established true.

LXX

At this young druggist Wenfield Pence's trial
fer his life,
On *primy faishy* evidence o' pizonin' his
wife,
Doc's testimony saved and cle'red and 'quitted
him and freed
Him so 's he never even 'peared cog-*ni*zant
of the deed!

LXXI

The facts wuz — Sifers testified,— at inquest he
had found
The stummick showed the woman *died* o'
pizon, but had downed
The dos't *herse'f*,— because *amount* and *cost*
o' drug imployed
No *druggist* would, on *no* account, a-lavished
and distroyed!

LXXII

Doc tracked a blame-don burgler down, and
nailed the scamp, to boot,
But told him ef he 'd leave the town he
would n't prosecute.
He traced him by a tied-up thumb-print in
fresh putty, where
Doc glazed it. Jes *that 's* how he come to
track him to his lair!

LXXIII

Doc 's jes a *leetle* too inclined, *some* thinks,
to overlook
The criminal and vicious kind we 'd ort to
bring to book
And punish, 'thout no extry show o' *sympa-
thizin'*, where
They hain't showed none fer *us*, you know.
But he takes issue there:

LXXIV

Doc argies 'at "The Red-eyed Law," as *he*
says, "ort to learn
To lay a mighty leenient paw on deeds o' sich
concern
As only the Good Bein' knows the wherefore
of, and spreads
HIS hands above accused and sows His mer-
cies on their heads."

LXXV

Doc even holds 'at *murder* hain't no crime we got a right
To *hang* a man fer—claims it 's *taint* o' *lunacy*, er *quite*.—
"Hold *sich* a man responsibul fer murder," Doc says,—"then,
When *he* 's hung, where 's the rope to pull them *sound-mind* jurymen?

LXXVI

"It 's in a nutshell—*all* kin see," says Doc,—"it 's cle'r the *Law* 's
As ap' to err as you er me, and kill without a cause:
The man most innocent o' sin *I* 've saw, er '*spect* to see,
Wuz servin' a life-sentence in the penitentchury."

LXXVII

And Doc 's a whole hand at a *fire!*—directin'
how and where
To set your ladders, low er higher, and what
first duties air,—
Like formin' warter-bucket-line; and best man
in the town
To chop holes in old roofs, and mine defec-
tive chimblies down:

LXXVIII

Er durin' any public crowd, mass-meetin', er
big day,
Where ladies ort n't be allowed, as I 've heerd
Sifers say,—
When they 's a suddent rush somewhere, it 's
Doc's voice, ca'm and cle'r,
Says, "Fall back, men, and give her air!—
that 's all she 's faintin' fer."

LXXIX

The sorriest I ever feel fer Doc is when some show
Er circus comes to town and he 'll not git a chance to go.
'Cause he jes natchurly *de*lights in circuses—clean down
From tumblers, in their spangled tights, to trick-mule and Old Clown.

LXXX

And ever'body *knows* it, too, how Doc is, thataway! . . . .
I mind a circus onc't come through — wuz there myse'f that day.—
Ringmaster cracked his whip, you know, to start the ridin'—when
In runs Old Clown and hollers "*Whoa!* — Ladies and gentlemen

LXXXI

"Of this vast audience, I fain would make in*qui*ry cle'r,
And learn, find out, and ascertain — *Is Doctor Sifers here?*"
And when some fool-voice bellers down: "He is! He 's settin' in
Full view o' ye!" "*Then*," says the Clown, "*the circus may begin!*"

LXXXII

Doc 's got a *temper;* but, he says, he 's
learnt it which is boss,
Yit has to *watch* it, more er less. . . . I
never seen him cross
But onc't, enough to make him swear;—
milch-cow stepped on his toe,
And Doc ripped out "*I doggies!*"—There 's
the only case I know.

LXXXIII

Doc says that 's what your temper 's fer—
to hold back out o' view,
And learn it never to occur on out ahead o'
you.—
"*You* lead the way," says Sifers—"git your
temper back in line—
And *furdest* back the *best,* ef it 's as mean a
one as mine!"

LXXXIV

He hates contentions — can't abide a wrangle
er dispute
O' any kind; and he 'ull slide out of a crowd
and skoot
Up some back-alley 'fore he 'll stand and
listen to a furse
When ary one 's got upper-hand and t' other
one 's got worse.

LXXXV

Doc says: "I 'spise, when pore and weak and
awk'ard talkers fails,
To see it 's them with hardest cheek and loud-
est mouth prevails. —
A' all-one-sided quarr'l 'll make me *biased*,
mighty near, —
'Cause ginerly the side I take 's the one I
never hear."

LXXXVI

What 'peals to Doc the most and best is "seein' folks *agreed*,
And takin' ekal interest and universal heed
O' ever'body *else 's* words and idies—same as we
Wuz glad and chirpy as the birds—jes as we 'd *ort* to be!"

LXXXVII

And *paterotic!* Like to git Doc started, full and fair,
About the war, and why 't 'uz fit, and what wuz 'complished there;
"And who wuz *wrong*," says Doc, "er *right*, 't 'uz waste o' blood and tears,
All prophesied in *Black* and *White* fer years and years and years!"

LXXXVIII

And then he 'll likely kind o' tetch on old John
Brown, and dwell
On what *his* warnin's wuz; and ketch his
breath and cough, and tell
On down to Lincoln's death. And *then*—
well, he jes chokes and quits
With "I must go now, gentlemen!" and grabs
his hat, and *gits!*

LXXXIX

Doc's own war-rickord wuz n't won so much
in line o' fight
As line o' work and nussin' done the wownded,
day and night.—
His wuz the hand, through dark and dawn, 'at
bound their wownds, and laid
As soft as their own mother's on their for-
reds when they prayed. . . .

XC

His wuz the face they saw the first—all dim, but smilin' bright,
As they come to and knowed the worst, yit saw the old *Red-White-*
And-Blue where Doc had fixed it where they 'd see it *wavin'* still,
Out through the open tent-flap there, er 'cros't the winder-sill.

XCI

And some 's a-limpin' round here yit—a-waitin' Last Review,—
'U'd give the pensions 'at they git, and pawn their crutches, too,
To he'p Doc out, ef he wuz pressed financial'—same as he
Has *allus* he'pped them when distressed—ner never tuk a fee.

XCII

Doc never wuz much hand to pay attention
    to *p'tence*
And fuss-and-feathers and display in men o'
    prominence:
"A railly *great* man," Sifers 'lows, "is not the
    out'ard dressed—
All uniform, salutes and bows, and swellin'
    out his chest.

XCIII

"I *met* a great man onc't," Doc says, "and shuk his hand," says he,
"And *he* come 'bout in *one*, I guess, o' dis-app'intin' *me*—
He talked so common-like, and brought his mind so cle'r in view
And simple-like, I purt'-nigh thought, '*I 'm* best man o' the two!'"

XCIV

Yes-*sir!* Doc 's got convictions and old-fashioned kind o' ways
And idies 'bout this glorious Land o' Freedom; and he 'll raise
His hat clean off, no matter where, jes ever' time he sees
The Stars and Stripes a-floatin' there and flappin' in the breeze.

XCV

And tunes like old "Red, White and Blue" 'll
fairly drive him wild,
Played on the brass band, marchin' through
the streets! Jes like a child
I 've saw that man, his smile jes set, all kind o'
pale and white,
Bare-headed, and his eyes all wet, yit dancin'
with delight!

XCVI

And yit, that very man we see all trimbly,
pale and wann,
Give him a case o' *surgery*, we 'll see another
man! —
We 'll do the trimblin' then, and *we* 'll git
white around the gills —
He 'll show us *nerve* o' nerves, and he 'ull show
us *skill* o' skills!

XCVII

Then you could toot your horns and beat
your drums and bang your guns,
And wave your flags and march the street,
and charge, all Freedom's sons! —
And Sifers *then*, I bet my hat, 'u'd never flinch
a hair,
But, stiddy-handed, 'tend to that pore patient
layin' there.

XCVIII

And Sifers' *eye* 's as stiddy as that hand o'
his! — He 'll shoot
A' old-style rifle, like he has, and smallest
bore, to boot,
With any fancy rifles made to-day, er expert
shot
'At works at shootin' like a *trade* — and all
some of 'em 's got!

XCIX

Let 'em go right out in the *woods* with Doc, and leave their "traps"
And blame glass-balls and queensware-goods, and see how Sifers draps
A squirrel out the tallest tree.—And 'fore he fires he 'll say
Jes where he 'll hit him—yes, sir-*ee!* And he 's hit thataway!

C

Let 'em go out with him, i jucks! with fishin'-pole and gun,—
And ekal chances, fish and ducks, and take the *rain*, er *sun*,
Jes as it pours, er as it blinds the eye-sight; *then*, I guess,
'At they 'd acknowledge, in their minds, their disadvantages.

CI

And yit *he 'd* be the last man out to flop his
wings and crow
Insultin'-like, and strut about above his fallen
foe!—
No-*sir!* the hand 'at tuk the wind out o'
their sails 'ud be
The very first they grabbed, and grinned to
feel sich sympathy.

CII

Doc gits off now and then and takes a huntin'-
trip somewhere
'Bout Kankakee, up 'mongst the lakes—some-
times 'll drift round there
In his canoe a week er two; then paddle clean
on back
By way o' old Wabash and Blue, with fish—
all he kin pack,—

CIII

And wild ducks—some with feathers on 'em
yit, and stuffed with grass.
And neighbers—all knows he 's bin *gone*—
comes round and gits a bass—
A great big double-breasted "rock," er "black,"
er maybe *pair*
Half fills a' ordinary crock. . . . Doc's *fish* 'll
give out there

CIV

Long 'fore his *ducks!*—But folks 'll smile and
blandish him, and make
Him tell and *tell* things!—all the while enjoy
'em jes fer sake
O' pleasin' *him;* and then turn in and la'nch
him from the start
A-tellin' all the things ag'in they railly know
by heart.

CV

He 's jes a *child*, 's what Sifers is! And-
sir, I 'd ruther see
That happy, childish face o' his, and puore
simplicity,
Than any shape er style er plan o' mortals
otherwise —
With perfect faith in God and man a-shinin'
in his eyes.

TAMÁM.

www.ingramcontent.com/pod-product-compliance
Lightning Source LLC
LaVergne TN
LVHW021422110826
845150LV00007B/2038

* 9 7 8 1 4 2 5 5 0 8 5 9 3 *